LINGUISTIC

FORMULA

$$A + F = L$$

MEXICO

Desegregated identity

By David Europa

LINGUISTIC FORMULA

Copyright © 2016 by David Ramirez - Europa

Library of Congress Control Number: 2016950818
ISBN-13: Paperback: 978-1-68256-850-7
          PDF: 978-1-68256-851-4
          ePub: 978-1-68256-852-1
          Kindle: 978-1-68256-853-8

Printed in the United States of America

LitFire LLC
1-800-511-9787
www.litfirepublishing.com
order@litfirepublishing.com

Contents

INTRODUCTION

ALPHABET+PHONOLOGY=LANGUAGE

$$A+F=L$$

(F and PH sound equal, F is used as simplification)

MEXICANO

To write, to read, to talk or to initiate any type of communication, the alphabet has to be utilized and the phonology will be the difference to recognize the identity of an individual.

This formula is to obtain the name of the language of every country employing the Alphabet imprinted as a validated document to support an economy.

Many words are written the same way in multiple Languages but the pronunciation is identifiable.

Example
-Natural, Multiple, Ritual, Royal, Fauna, Flora, Material

Some continent's name
-America, Africa, Asia, Antartica, Australia

OBJECTIVE OF THIS MANUSCRIPT.

The only purpose of this manuscript is the desegregation of an individual born in territory of Mexico, generation 1972 from Hispanic, Latino or Mexican to present his unique identity as Mexicano, introducing his own Language (Lenguaje Mexicano or Lengua Mexicana) utilizing a Linguistic Formula (A+F=L) I Speak words using the alphabet plus my accent makes me be identified as Mexicano with own music, folklore, culinary art and many dissimilar characteristics from people of all the countries around the world.

Alphabet+Phonology=MEXICANO

MY IDENTITY

In Tenochtitlan, Nahuatl used to
be talked by the Aztecs in the Market
they built to control and organize any miss
transaction to not interrupt the activities in
what later was called City.

Aztec seem to be the final result from
Aztlan or Aztlalteca and many more words
that were being absorbed by the movement,
technics, skills and multiple faculties
they counted with to detect anomalies in
quantity, size or weight of the merchandise
purchase.

The chosen territory was already
inhabited by groups of people creating their
own tools and instruments to manufacture
all was needed to ignite a civilization. The
only available space to build the market to

connect different routes of commerce was over the lagoon to produce the quantity of food as they were growing.

According to the arriving people from Europe with long beard, riding horses, three ships and their final conclusion was a suppose Conquest by the version in Spanish and now translated in different Languages.

In this Version, the explanation will be focus on how the initiators of the Tenochtitlan's Market decided to hire that group of people to reach even farer horizons and accept their administrative labor and the transactions between them and whoever was persecuting them, to help them earn properties and important titles and names to go back to their regions with the equivalence to reenter in their monarchical rituals. Wherever they brought, gave remarkable result with the objective they were looking for to the point where they couldn't produce an efficient technology to maintain a stabilized economy. Suddenly they started to decay and face a voracious territorial snatching from the Nation of USA and now, the territory called Mexico has an embarrassing situation, deteriorating my identity.

By the 1870's Mexico declared war against Spain which never confronted and USA reporters recorded to prove the battle between Mexicanos and Hispanics born in Mexico. Once Villa and Zapata toke the presidency, they told them to keep administrating if that was what they wanted to help to the point where USA snatched part of the territory due to the deficit the Spanish administration had with them.

All the revolutionary battle was for the territory of Mexico and our education.

Many images posted on the internet show how Revolutionary groups were executing defenseless indigenous. This Revolutionary groups were probably saying to stop calling Spanish to the spoken language at that time but they just couldn't present their complete desegregation either.

Prove

Video posted on the internet describing the dispute for Mexico's territory.

-The Storm that Swept Mexico.

Before the end of 2012 I posted on Facebook the prediction according to the Aztecs to be the end of the "WORLD" and I posted my Linguistic Formula on Photos saying the following

By the end of 2012 the WORLD will end.

I understand

PLANET as the rotating mass orbiting the sun 93 million miles
away.

WORLD where the human been races interact as a population with the faculty to comprehend the actual situation and activities develop.

Then I reposted on Facebook "Alphabet+Phonology=Language" In addition, this manuscript as book with the introduction of my own Language in my own version as Mexicano before any prediction occurred.

CONTINENTS AND COUNTRIES

The countries in America, Europe, Africa and Asia are organized in a single continent each. Many of this countries have the privilege to exclaim the name of their own Language according to their nationality. Others say the same utilizing English Language consequently, those territories containing groups of people don't have a Language.

Prove in Europe

-England - English

-Germany - German

-France - French

-Spain - Spanish

-Portugal - Portuguese

-Ireland - English from "England"

-Denmark - English from "England"

In Asia

China -   Chinese in English by Americans.
           (Chinese Symbols are thoughts)

Japan - Japanese written in English

In Africa the countries speak their
languages as ethnic communication, using
English Language to obtain a salary and
participate in events.

Angola - Portuguese written in English by Americans

In America three Languages, American English, Spanish and some French after a massive immigration from all over the planet conquest

Brazil - Portuguese in English by Americans and because a Portuguese person discovered it according to natives in the actuality.

Mexico - According to the benefit of many people and organizations around the world Spanish is the official Language to permit individuals to enter to an administrative way to semi live. All the population immigrating to USA from South America speaks and imitates the accent from Mexico and the whole vocabulary, admitting Spanish as their Mother Language as well. They call to themselves Hispanics, Latinos and Mexicans.

Hispanic - Mass of people admitting Spanish as their Mother
                        Language

Latino - Mix between White men and Black woman to stop Slavery.

Mexican - A secondary identity prevenient from Mexicanos to be classified in a system and translation.

Also, Mexico has had different names such as New Spain to claim the territory as part of Spain, then after years, the country was called Mexico only. All this change was made by individuals born in Mexico for the prosperity of the people with the Identity corresponding to Mexico with Sombrero.

A suppose conquest from Spain to a territory still not called Mexico or America was propagated allowing people to obtain land, money and power. This version was told by Europeans after seeing part of their population escaping away from their regiments to put in practice all they learned in those regiments. Administration was part of that learning, this way, the Aztec market was implemented with another image to bring even more visitor to share investigations, society solutions and ways to recognize inventions for a better living way.

Mexico for many mean Mix (mix of races)

Mexico is equal to Fusion which is the only way a new generation can obtain faculties from one side of the family and features from the other one.

Example
A salad dish (mix) can be mixed with multiple ingredients, if the same salad is made without one ingredient, the dish continuous being a salad.

A shake (fusion) is made with milk, fruit, sugar, eggs and once is blended, the only way this ingredients can be separated is through humans body system.

-Mexicano is from Mexico
-Mexican is from outside Mexico

If Mexicano corresponds to Mexico
and I am Mexicano proving to speak
my own Language using the alphabet
and pronouncing it my way, I am the only
proprietary of the territory of Mexico.

USA - American English the Language
is called now, incorporating words from
different regions to enrich the vocabulary
according to the working field. With a big
percentage of the vocabulary, the people
from USA emphasize them in a different
pronunciation to exhibit their nationality.

American English is a Mercantile
Language.

Example

McDonald's Restaurant sells Hamburgers (recipe) all over the world obtaining productivity from their investment as a franchise administrated by Americans.

GUACAMOLE is a recipe from Mexico, alphabetized to place it on a menu to invite guests to taste our culinary art, administrated by Hispanics.

GRINGO, GREEN GO when people from Mexico's territory saw men approaching, wearing green military uniform, supposedly coming from war, asking for free food, told them this way to show unwelcome manner.

DISTINCTION BETWEEN AMERICA AND REST OF THE WORLD

The only way to identify the pronunciation in many words is creating a new letter from "t" and "r?

Water, Peter, Butter, Property, Administrative, Enchilada

In American English, American Dream
is money and the only way to obtain it
is understanding the system which is
working, studying, reading to tell ideas for
implementation.

WHAT A LANGUAGE GENERATES.

New words to represent an identity in a economical organization

IMPERICOUS - Masculine

IMPERESSE - Feminine

In other places with English as Official Language

King - Queen

President - First Lady

AMERICAN MYTHOLOGY

A Mexicano (Mehecano) from outside the wall came unidentified but helped by his three respective Gods to face a Territorial Duel containing a double Language to obtain the privilege to marry The Fifty Stars most beautiful woman from The America Dream's Kingdom.

-Three Respective Gods-

ATRAKALLOUS - From Mexicano "Atracar" to disable.

AMMAGALLOUS - From Mexicano "Amagar" to embrace.

AKABALLOUS - From Mexicano "Acabar" to finish.

The Three Mysterious Gods some night talked to a man to present him the only possibility to obtain the America's Fifty Stars most beautiful woman to marry him. As long he utilizes the meaning of The Three Mysterious God names to triumph against the inclemency of a distinct Language reigned by The Mortal God "TAFOOOOOOOOOK".

TAFOK - Extremely Furious Mortal God formed by the accumulation of knowledge, pressure, disorder, abuse and rage to fight against the promise land seekers to help them find what they were looking for to send them back to their destiny saved. TAFOK was sent mortal in order to procreate his pure precious daughter, the fifty stars beautiful woman to rule after TAFOK's death to branch out his legacy.

TAFOK - From American phrase "to be furious"

According to all TAFOK was standing out to and defeating everything on his path, his main concern was the man his daughter was going to marry and why if he was expecting someone with the right credentials, the same skin color and mentality from his own territory he obtained himself by every law and right of the universe to keep his personal business alive.

Meanwhile, Resucito Villa first pure immortal son of the God VILLAINOUS from the next town down the Americas already in TAFOK's territory; absorbed

by the real well compensated living way
after getting certified and executing his
skills to earn money and all knocked out
was confronting the devastation of his land
showing the cruel defense of TAFOK
over any matter to deal with. His highest
level of education was his own identity,
preserved in music and folklore, achieving
a Kitchen Manager charge and indecisive
future.

Days and nights Resucito (Resucitto)
struggled with misunderstandings over the
spoken language at work without alternative
but to report it to a recognized agency
to take over the big problem the linguistic
matter was creating at the edge of his
penumbral life.

VERSIFIED THOUGHT

I PREFER
TO RISK
MY LIFE
AND MY LIBERTY,
RATHER
TO LOSE
MY IDENTITY.

"MEXICANO"

David Europa

DIFFERENCES BETWEEN

MEXICANO -   HISPANIC,
              LATINO
              MEXICAN.

During many decades, people from
Mexico has been called illegal,
undocumented, wetback and nicknames to
damage the identity. For many mistakes
made by Hispanics, Latinos or Mexicans,
my person as Mexicano has to suffer the
consequences.

MEXICANO

-Independence is never in my celebrations.
- The root of my Language comes from commerce in what now is called America.
-Military Heritage
      "Azteca, Villista, Zapatista, Ramirez
      Europa"
-God (Di-os) is the simplification or reduction from two words
"Tell Us"
Tell - Di   Us - nosotros
              Di-Nos = Dios
when the desperation to know where to go, forced the believers to ask, giving up to any alternative for the right path.
-God (Dios) is a compound inside of our anatomy to comprehend life in a constructive way for the benefit of humanity.
-Fusion is the way I am form.
- Jesus is a reference BC/AC

-Antichrist is against cruelty.

HISPANIC, LATINO or MEXICAN

-Evolution produces violence in their head.
For not reason they
want to fight as they want to take
properties from others.
-God (Dios) is The Creator, The
Almighty, The Powerful and more.
-They don't know what Independence is.
-Is a mix from nomad races, situated in what
now is called South America.
-Call Spanish to what they talk for the
believe of a conquest.
-Lie when they presume have studied
something by just obtaining a certificate to
obtain a job which they only use to ruin the

image and identity of the people from their own country.

-Their best contribution to the world is their very valuable and accessible workforce.

-Promotes the consume of bad quality products.

-Mitigate their charlatanry in presence of a foreign person.

-Jesus is the image of a cruelly punished individual seen as their savior and yet, they still have to go to Church to confess their sins.

-Antichrist is the Devil, Satan, Lucifer.

AMERICA.

America in the actuality has two functions, one is a Country and the other is a Continent.

The name of America was taken from the Navigator Amerigo Vespucci (Americo Vespucio in Mexico) to be modified and alphabetized as AMERICA to take it as reference to know where items and valuables were going to end. This way AMERICA was named as the Market to create commerce with people from Europe after knowing they were going to return for more material, ideas, item's collection, food and the most important, money.
This way, Spanish was hired to deal with them if they knew how to handle their own people unknowingly igniting Independence.

According to all the Languages, America was Discovered by Columbus.

-How did he know the land was called America if they were lost?

Difference between America's Market Initiators and European Versions.

-AMERICA'S MARKET INITIATORS.

WE "NAMED IT AMERICA"

At that time, the Aztec Civilization was dominating and new generations from Emperors with high authority women from other civilizations they married were modifying the vocabulary and accent as well.

-EUROPEAN VERSION

They "CALLED AMERICA" after hearing the new word to know where they can go to invest their studies, formulas and inventions.

America for all this, is the market where money has to be in every individual to pay for all the needs and likes.

The word AMERICA is not English or Spanish. People from all over the world learned how to pronounce it.

AMERICA'S THEORY

The unborn daughter Vespucci didn't want to have in this territory to be in charge of all his intentions, in addition, Languages

from what now is called Continent of
Europe were not recognized yet.

AMERICA as distortion.

Is the pronunciation's distortion of the
word (name) "Amerigo" in feminine gender,
for then, take it as the name of the market
in multiple Languages.
English, Spanish, Portuguese, French
and now "Mexicano"

AMERICAN

Who is American?

-A person with black skin color saying he/
she is African-American born in USA
talking English, asking for money on the
streets as homeless?

-AFRORICAN?

-A person with Asian features imitating the accent from USA and not English from England saying his nationality is Japanese, Chinese just born in USA?

-A white person from Polish, Irish or German parents running away from their bombarded countries?

-The result from Indian mother and Mexican father just talking English and superficial Spanish?

-Italian, Irish, Mexican, Polish single daughter?

-Some adopted boy from Malaysia after losing his parents?

-A man from Mexico without English at all and just by summiting an application after the eighteen years of waiting for his daughter to claim him?

-An Estadounidense?

AMERICAN to my understanding is the wise white man born in the USA territory inventing and formulating the way to obtain the best benefit from projects to know the human been origin and the only ones making that to happen are the known White people with the capacity to make real any idea to comprehend the meaning of our nature and appearance in this life. In the actuality scientist, astronauts and employees of gigantic organizations such as NASA have come from different regions around the planet to take advantage of the facilities already established and founded by white people born in USA to somehow obtain territory to extract material needed for technology. Facilities cinematographically promoting movie stars to promote the aspect of a person from around the world founded by White people born in USA. Professional Sport

Facilities to exploit the faculty of an individual to be classified over many more unfortunate people, built and organized by White people and multiple organizations supported by White people because they read everything to know the cause of any matter.

EXPERIENCE WITH HISPANICS.

-During my adolescent life in school, with
people from Spain we were classmates
which they always questioned me why I
speak Spanish if I am not from Spain?
I replied because that's the Official
Language for now.

-My paternal grandfather was an employed
in a wholesale market in Mexico City.
His labor was to sell spices in mass (a
representative), making a lot of money by
his skills to sell. He never used a bank as
a security option, instead, he decided to
give the administration of his own money
to his bosses (people from Spain). After
years, obviously he was getting older and he
needed someone to keep that job for more

generations. One day I went with him to be introduced as his grandson who was going to take over his job once I have learned all the methods.

The meeting was like a clash. They talk to me in their accent and I responded with my accent without hesitation with the most respectful manner. I had the opportunity to go with my grandfather only three times, after that, I was told to stay at home with no explanation at all.

-At work, in a hotel, I used to serve in the bar area. The General Manager, a person from Spain, was promoted with this position after his trajectory in the corporation as Electrical Technician. His attitude became aggressive and sarcastic. My discontent led me to imitate what others were doing, braking glasses, bottles, equipment with

extreme negligence while the General
Manager was not present, bringing women
to his office even in the busiest nights.
After a few days, I was called to come to
the General Manager's office. Once in the
office, another employee was already there.
With this coworker, we were like partners
at work, he even invited me to his home
with the others to take a beer, instead, he
stayed silenced, not even tried to look at
me, suddenly, the General Manager arrived.
He invited us to seat down while he was
preparing his plan.

G. M.- We have known by this person
        next to you that from our business,
        you are trying to open another
        one on your own by selling
        drinks and bottles to our clients.
He asked to the other employee

G. M.- Is it true that David Ramirez
Europa is selling drinks
and bottles to our clients
clandestinely?
without hesitation he responded
only
Employee- "Yes"
abstaining himself to not say another word.
When I looked at him, he was shaking his
hands, then I turned to tell the General
Manager in a solid manner. I didn't become
exalted.
David - I just come here to work.
He incremented the penalty pronouncing
G. M. that's a criminal case and you can go
to prison for a long time.
Once again, in a normal expression, I
aggregated
David - "I don't care if he accuses me and
you think that of me.

The General Manager just fired me in a worst manner than a Patron. This way I had to get out of my own country as soon as possible to avoid more threatening from this person and his friends.

-One time, a person representing a touristic trips to Europe offered me a package to go to Spain and Italy with many attractions included but I had to use another name because David Ramirez Europa was not credible, deciding to cancel.

-In Mexico, visitors from South America with very amply vocabulary in Spanish approach to me to throw at me their complains about the type of life existing in there as they had the authority to say anything just for traveling as tourist.

-In USA, since I got to the City of
Chicago, I have sent my resume to the
culinary and hospitality fields applying for
the lowest qualification I think I have as Line
Cook, previously I was a Kitchen Manager.
As the responsible of a kitchen, I have
learned if we run out of employees, I have
to do everything I can count with to not fail
such as sweep and mop floor, preparation
for the ingredients we need for the menu's
recipes or wash dishes, to this point
everything is fine with not complains, but
when the Chef is 27 years old, expecting
every station with some body to handle
tickets supervised by his Sous Chef and
during five or six days without dishwasher
person with a ninety percent Hispanic,
Latino or Mexican, feeling compelled
to handle two station and the Chef with
nomad features American English talker,
walking around the kitchen chatting on the

phone, showing me pictures with coworkers having fun the previous night, I couldn't resist to thank for the opportunity of working in that kitchen.

By having obtained over four certification I wanted to try out another region in the States, different working platform, more money and more risky social life. Thinks went wrong for me, economy slowed down momentarily, forcing me to return to Chicago IL. The way I started to explain people the reason of not wanting to be considered as Hispanic was causing problems with them, for me, I was suffering a transition to understand better what I wanted to achieve.

Newly, I insisted sending my resume to different restaurants, Bistros, Italian & pizza Osteria and what I always was trying

to avoid, in a Taco's Restaurant, one of
the employees there, a feminine, started
smiling at me, in a few more visits, we had
the chance to cross some words without
letting go the opportunity to tell her
she was so beautiful and her eyes were
even more. She run away, continuing with
her job. the next visits, the encounters
were more friendly to the point I had to
invite her out for a lunch which she didn't
answer. I wrote a few lines to tell her how
beauty she was to me and gave them to
her the next visit. I always was busy with
just minutes to swallow food, I didn't have
enough time to talk to her for over one or
two minutes. I decided to write down all my
status information, address, phone number
to let her know about me after I saw police
officers walking in and out the restaurant,
thinking she probably knew them to give
her confidence if she was interested as well.

Definitely I couldn't have time to at least asker to be my girlfriend or something like that. I stop visiting the restaurant and when a month past, I had to renew the State Identification. At the Secretary of the State of Illinois, the clerk reopens multiple times my information page on the computer, she turned the monitor to let me see the name and all my information didn't match with the number I was presenting. The Social Security Office clerk told me the same thing.

Somehow I got a job in a restaurant, a Chef I knew was having an open call for back of the house getting hired to start within the next ten days. Everything was going very well until when the Sous Chef from outside USA one day came to me asking me for tasks supposed to be completed earlier with over boss manner, asking me why I always had to answer him

back with a serious face with his finger
pointing at me near two inches from my
face, I responded I didn't know about
that. After a few minutes, he came to me
with the General Manager, pointing at me
saying this has to be suspended. Rapidly,
another Sous Chef found me to talk to
the other Sous chef the three of us only
in the office, he was there working on the
computer, the other Chef let me in first
and when he turned to see who was coming,
furiously got up from the chair to grab the
door and slam it to my face. I stopped the
door with my food, he said to the other,
he has to go forcing the other to take me
away, I said the Chef told me to stay here
and I won't move, then the Sous Chef
got even frustrated by didn't know what to
do. I just walked away, at home I email the
Corporation's Manager in New York to
inform about the incident. The next day

the Chef replied to have a meeting at my arriving. The Chef, the General Manager and I gather at a table to give my version. The General Manager pacified the situation and I understood very well, with the Sous Chef, we shacked hands and continued working as nothing happened. Soon, a person from South America was hired. It didn't pass a week when he started commenting me his experience with women from Mexico and the way he thinks about people from them. I listened to him but not answer to avoid problems or fights. He was a very short man almost midget but with a big mouth, fearing to say all the people from Mexico are wet backs, undocumented and more. I had to go find the Sous Chef to inform him about his comments. He was taken out the kitchen and didn't return for the rest of the night. At home I mailed to the Chef to inform about it and present him a two week notice. The cook was fire and I returned to work the following day. By opting to stop talking to the Hispanics, Latinos and Mexicans to avoid problems, I was criticized as racist for not talking to my own people. I explained my reason to one of the Sous Chefs to clarify my posture. Once again, things when wrong, the two week notice time ended, I thanked to the Chef and applied in another food market.

Until here, I was visited, interviewed and staged in at least ten restaurants quitting and running away to not fall into a fight to avoid police solution according to my linguistic comments.

Another beautiful restaurant with a Chef from Italy supposedly. The Chef

didn't wear uniform cooking or not, he
always wanted to speak Spanish because
that's what he thought they talked. This
time people from Mexico and South
America infested the kitchen united
to the vulgar vocabulary that was out of
control. Before the Great Opening, the
Chef cooked for the responsible group
of that new business; I dared to say they
should've thrown two hundred dollars to let
him get a uniform which I paid myself for just
a pair of shoes and a pair of cooking pants.
One of the Sous Chef was near me and
he heard my comment, the following day, the
Chef was a little more organized uniformly
and serious when he looked at me. Training
days past and the Great Opening was a
fiasco with a reservation list of no more than
thirty guests. One day I commented how we
had to present the dish or cook it to follow

the Chef's instructions. Another cooking equipment arrived to that kitchen and when we had the opportunity to use it, when I was going to place a fish on the surface, he snatched it from my hands to show how to do it. I didn't want to wait until the end of the night to quit.

I was hired after three interviews, the Chef was a very nice person and supervising all the kitchens. Half of the employees were Hispanics and with some of them I clearly told them not to call me the same way they call to everybody with the same words. They didn't care continuing with the same offensive vocabulary. After I decided to completely ignore them, stop talking to they just to ask for what we needed to cook or prepare. This time, I had a chat with another Sous Chef and

a floor Manager. They told me about my
behavior with the rest of the employees;
I told them the same thing I told to the
Hispanics, they seemed to be satisfied with
a few comments we crossed concluding with
another two week notice.

This employer offered me Health
and Dental benefits which I accepted. As
soon I received the card, I went online to
look for a nearby Dental location. From
three adds I decided to pick a Hispanic
Health Help. Days later, at the location,
the doctor interviewed me, I clearly let
him know I had a limited coverage up to a
thousand dollars, no worries and hospitality
was performed; following the requirements
to determine my mouth was in ruins needing
a lot of work. As I like to wear black color, in
my next visit, I was wearing black color but
this time I brought shorts and sneakers. In
the first visit, the doctor again was wearing

the classic nurse uniform in complete pink
fabric. By the third and last visit, the doctor
was wearing complete black uniform like
to imitating me. That day the doctor told
me I needed mouth cleaning with a service
duration of forty five minutes, I agreed and
I med another doctor. On the chair, she
started working on my denture, I close my
eyes while listening music from my phone
to not be staring at her, after the end of a
six or seven minutes of a video, suddenly
the doctor told me !almost done! I opened
my eyes, she got up to grab a plastic
bag with tooth paste, a toothbrush and
brochures. At home, I decided to email
the Dental office to let them know about
the cancelation of my treatment. I paid
the amount they showed me. I searched on
the internet again finding a location in a
higher class neighborhood. This time the
doctor was an Indian person born in USA.

I explained the experience with the other doctor and the coverage limit I had; she toke my case to start the treatment. She called to the other Dental location to transfer all my information. She explained me I needed a lot of work but not worries about the limits because she was going to try to not go over to save me money. The first bill was close to fourteen hundred dollars; I paid half of that amount to not minimize the next payments. By the last visit the doctor showed me a bigger amount of money after my mouth had a dental extraction on one side, the need of a crown with the work incomplete and a broken tooth by her negligence when she was hammering to find sensitive areas in a bad manner. The next visit I just missed it to not fall in arguments. I email the Dental office to explained the situation and the doctor just tried to offer me a discount if I wanted her to continue working on my mouth. Due the email I sent to the Office, the Doctor's husband called me on my phone to tell me why I caused to his wife and anything related to her, he was the responsible to face it. I answered back that his best action to take was to call the police and Hanged up on him. At night, once again I email the Dental office to let them know about the phone called from the doctor's husband. No more phone calls or emails were needed.

No longer than two weeks, I had to stop working after I told to one of the Hispanic food runners if I was doing something wrong, just tell the Chef to correct it. Some of the runners went to the Manager, I saw the Manager and the Chef conversation looking at me. In a few more minutes, the Chef changed his attitude towards me. I didn't want to find out by the end of the night the reason, just informed to another Sous Chef I had to leave because that was becoming a problem.

It toke me a few days to hear from another group of hotels and restaurants to stage in one of their kitchen to posteriorly get hired as line cook. Confrontations with Hispanic cooks and their friends couldn't wait against me. In one of the meetings I told the Chef two of the cooks were harassing when they try to decide what equipment I should've used or where to place resting meat or any details and he said I don't have to feel like that. By the preparation area, the space was very tight and one of the employees past by me hitting me with his shoulder as he wanted me to move away. Three or four hours of service past and once again, the same cook wanted to past by me trying to push me away. At the end of the night at home, I emailed the Chef to inform him about the incident culminating that day was my last day of labor there.

My linguistic topic couldn't stop forcing me to commented everywhere I went and went I got hired in another restaurant, thinking that my linguistic work was right, I told to many about my ideas which I was going to publish. They didn't believe anything at all, provoking bad comments and conflicts with many Hispanic cooks. Some of them were part of the preparation group and when I needed something for the list of dishes under my responsibility in Spanish they told me to ask to the Chef for anything I was going to need for my dishes. When I went to the Chef to ask for something he didn't believe me at all. I really didn't want to fall into their vocabulary game to not create friction and when a Hispanic

tried to play his vocabulary game with me,
I told him to stop talking to me, only asking
me for everything related to the restaurant,
not in Spanish and if I was doing something
wrong, the best thing to do was to inform
the Chef or call to the police; neither of
that past, they just created a comment
of I have a bipolar problem, I responded
they can think anything about me just
don't talk to me in Spanish and nothing
related to their ruined life. Every morning I
encountered the same preparation people;
one of them asked me in front of more cooks
how people from Mexico use a few words in
our country, I answer back with this...

Try to not ask me anything related
to the Spanish you think we speak, I
am saying that to write, to talk or to read
(A+F=L) to prove I speak Mexicano

disaggregated from what is called Spanish and what you have as vocabulary, is nothing but everything from Mexico if you haven't talked to a person from Spain in the flesh, he disliked my point of view and I added that's why I don't want to talk to you because you do not understand yet by not having at least one certification from USA or the place you came from.

    He got furious feeling to be offended. One of the Chefs saw one mourning how I didn't say hello to them, no comment came out from him and the time past in the same routine.
    Suddenly, another Sous Chef's confrontation. He talked to me sometimes and when I talked to him he ignored me completely, then I say hello to a coworker and he exclaimed mad with provoking

vocabulary. I replied if you think I am doing something wrong, call the police. A couple of days later, after having a busy brunch service, I cleaned my station for the night time cook, I helped the other cooks to put away container with label and date, sweep and mop the floor, organize the walking cooler consolidating containers to have more space. Just when I was trying to check out with the Chef he tried to order me to organize the equipment I was using. Every equipment was with the night time menu ingredients already and he couldn't say anything else, then I asked.

Do you want me to clean it up or just want me to seem doing something when you get here?

He didn't answered back. I emailed to the Chef my story telling him that when that person clocks in, I was going to grab

my tools to put them away and leave my
station as it was to avoid conflicts with
him, also I said I don't talk to him again.
No answer from the Chef and the next
day at the restaurant when the Sous Chef
got there, I informed to the mourning Sous
Chef about the email I sent to the Chef.
They chatted for a few minutes and we
tried to avoid each other.

One day before my final day there,
we had a busy brunch service, I kept the
same routine cleaning and organizing my
station. Again, the Sous Chef was trying
to find any mistake from my part to make
sure he was the boss there to new staging
cooks. I ignored him then I went to look for
the mourning Sous Chef to check out. The
following mourning I got the ingredients
list to start organizing my station. For
one recipe I found an two orders and a

half. I commented to another cook if that was going to be enough according to the weather and the reservation on the book; she agreed with me to tell the Sous Chef to tell the preparation cooks. Around nine in the morning I told the Chef we needed that ingredient by eleven o'clock, then lettuce for salad wasn't ready and when I ask to the preparation cooks for the lettuce, again they told me to inform the chef. Within the fifteen orders we got at once, many needed the ingredient I asked for earlier in the morning, when I run out of it, I told the Chef about it. I went down stairs to the main kitchen to ask for the ingredient, another Sous Chef responded it will be ready on ten minutes. The night time cooks saw me going back and forth multiple times asking for preparation. In a moment I saw the mourning Sous Chef conversing with

concerns. By two pm the Sous Chef to one of their offices. The room was empty, only the two of us,

Sous Chef- I think you are having problems with the preparation
            people
            and another Sous Chef.
David - When I tell you what I need, you don't believe me because
            you think what we have available will be enough to pass
            the lunch time and I don't come here to find problems,
            you see it that way is your point of view.
Sous Chef- Because I don't, I really don't believe you.
David- I have nothing to do here then. Thank you.
Sous Chef- (no words at all).

In a normal mode, I went to get my knife case, punch out, back down to the locker room, get changed; to the employees I saw I said good bye and just walking out the door, at the Patio, employees from that same restaurant were visiting as guest. I saw them but kept walking as I didn't see them, one of them, a lesbian person, someone whom I talked to about her sexual preferences and disagreeing with her when she exclaimed she was Mexican from Mexico. When I pass by their table, I saw this employee turning to say hello to me, I was wearing ear buds and I pretended to not hear anything, then one of her friends yelled something very loud in Spanish which I didn't understand to not even turn to see.

In the night, I email to the Chef the incident and said thanks to once again, quitting before a two week notice.

From all this mess, another employee from South America got near me to have a conversation about where I came from and transforming the conversation into a game to tall me

Employee- Honestly, I know you are from Mexico but don't you think
        people from Mexico are ignorant?
David- Why do you say that to me? get away from me and don't
        talk to me again.
        I really wanted to hit him with what I had in my hand (sauté pan) but I knew that was because all the Hispanics, Latinos and Mexicans.

        Why an individual none American, no identity and no language instead telling me he/she is the Chef, Doctor, Administrator for instance, has to tell me is my boss and I have to obey just because he/she speaks English?

Why after being hired and run away from different employers with a total of at least twenty five, this type of employee is allowed and not reported to the corresponding authorities?

For me, this's been a transition in my own person to comprehend openly my linguistic work.

Now at my address, a group of Chinese manage the building; the Chinese man wants me to talk to him only inside the house and outside he is going to ignore me as two different races but he

ask me to fix air conditioning and heating
appliances or problems with his automobile.
One of the Chinese woman occupying a
room in the first floor without English at all,
with signs only tried to complain to me the
neighbors don't let her sleep when they play
music in weekends celebrating a birthday or
a family reunion.

PERSONAL LIBERATION

America is a market
Market is an economy
Economy is the money I have to reinvest in
myself
I am the responsible for my own implement
Implement is every certification
Certification is a completed training
Training is needed to obtain a job
Job is the qualification to be trusted.

As long I am certified in different fields,
I will have the possibility to apply for the
job which will help me to form myself as a
positive individual to be admitted.

Infallible method.

When a person obtains at least six certification, will have multiple options to generate money, If this person starts failing in one field, it'll be the chance to try out another one because all those skills are an investment. If this person completely fails, will opt for robbery or anything against integrity which such action is nowhere tolerated.

PURPOSE OF THIS MANUSCRIPT.

      With this manuscript I want to claim all the productivity (Money) from all the recipes alphabetized in Mexico being profit in any Language, in any region and as my property, recipes such as Guacamole, Taco, Torta, Quesadilla, Pozole, Menudo, etc.

Why?

Because that's never been Spanish, the people just want to integrate it to it and those recipes are for Mexicanos to invite guest to taste our culinary art or cuisine.

Also Music.
Why Music?

Because many songs narrate the battle for our Identity as Mexicanos and singers sing them in concerts where they receive a pay check or percentage, in addition, if they admit Spanish as their Mother Language even though they were born in Mexico, with what purpose?

One of the most used instruments is the Guitar, made in Paracho, Michoacan called as Spanish Guitar because that state is located in Mexico where the whole world thinks is Spanish Property.

For me, every person saying is from Mexico, has to present at least six certification to comprehend the system to help them develop some idea for implementation.

-Who are they going to present it to?
-Why David I Ramirez Europa has
to "force" them to do that?
-Who is going to pay for that?

Now, after years of singing the
revolutionary song s with lyric including
in any possible way the word of Mexico,
the singers who were opted to earn the
money by presenting their suppose
tradition in Ranchero events, most of
them people born in Mexico. If those
songs were written by somebody else
and these singers past away, their new
family generations possibly will keep that
earning by simply saying

"those songs were for my father to sing
songs from the revolution"

this way, taking over all the monetary
transaction into their own bank account
and the worst to me, investing in programs
to force people to not renounce to their
Language which is Spanish.

WHY TO AVOID SPANISH IN MY BUSYNESS.

A big percentage of Hispanic, Latino or Mexicans do not have training from their own initiative to know what to do. With the Language they have as way of communication from the region they come from, is impossible to hear it every day.

CONCLUSION.

As Mexicano, I never have been under nobody's regiment, nor I have to inform the preferences of Languages I want to talk. I am subjected to investigate and to work to implement my identity.

REQUEST

The only reason I have been in the USA is to maintain my Linguistic Investigation to show evidence to present it to a USA authority to validate my claiming request of the territory of Mexico as my property and everything is generating to opt for a proper administration from the USA in the language it has to be utilized to keep my identity in a level a normal person will have the faculty to life with integrity.

In USA

Once this request is validated with a copyright number, every single individual exclaiming to be Mexicano will have the responsibility to present six certifications as minimum requirement in a hundred and eighty days, paid from their own bank account as the responsible of their own personal training implementation.

In Mexico

Inform the Government to get every person according to their age with six certifications presented in a hundred and eighty days to posteriorly, if they qualify, perform their training and to wear Sombrero.

David Europa.